RIDDLE BY THE RIVER

STORY BY **MARCIA VAUGHAN**

PICTURES BY **REYNOLD RUFFINS**

Silver Burdett Press

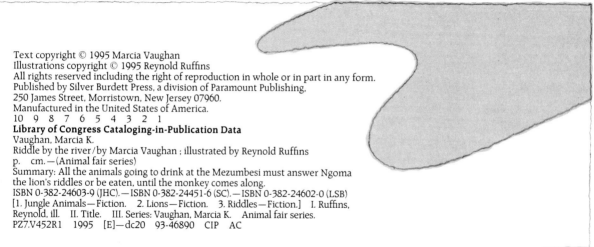

Published by Silver Burdett Press, a division of Paramount Publishing,
250 James Street, Morristown, New Jersey 07960.
Manufactured in the United States of America.
10 9 8 7 6 5 4 3 2 1
Library of Congress Cataloging-in-Publication Data
Vaughan, Marcia K.
Riddle by the river / by Marcia Vaughan ; illustrated by Reynold Ruffins
p.   cm. — (Animal fair series)
Summary: All the animals going to drink at the Mezumbesi must answer Ngoma
the lion's riddles or be eaten, until the monkey comes along.
ISBN 0-382-24603-9 (JHC). — ISBN 0-382-24451-6 (SC). — ISBN 0-382-24602-0 (LSB)
[1. Jungle Animals — Fiction.   2. Lions — Fiction.   3. Riddles — Fiction.]   I. Ruffins,
Reynold, ill.   II. Title.   III. Series: Vaughan, Marcia K.   Animal fair series.
PZ7.V452R1   1995   [E] — dc20   93-46890   CIP   AC

For Richard, who always has a song in his heart! — *M.V.*

For Rebecca and Ranger — *R.R.*

There is a river in Africa called the Galana. It is as curvy as a python, as brown as a hippo, and as long as forever. Each evening, as the sun melts into the sky, animals follow the path through the jungle to drink the cool brown water of the Galana.

In a cave at the edge of the path lived Ngoma, the lion. Ngoma was as old as the hills, as yellow as the sun, and as sly as a shadow.

One evening, Ngoma lay in the shade of the waitabit bush when...*krik-de, krik-de, krik-de*...springing down the jungle path came cricket.

"Tell me, Jimjup," Ngoma purred, "where are you going on this sun-hot evening?"

"Down to the Galana to drink the cool water," Jimjup answered. "All day I've been leaping from lizards. I am very thirsty."

Ngoma strolled out and sat on the path. "Do you like riddles, Jimjup?"

"Oh, yes," chirped the cricket.

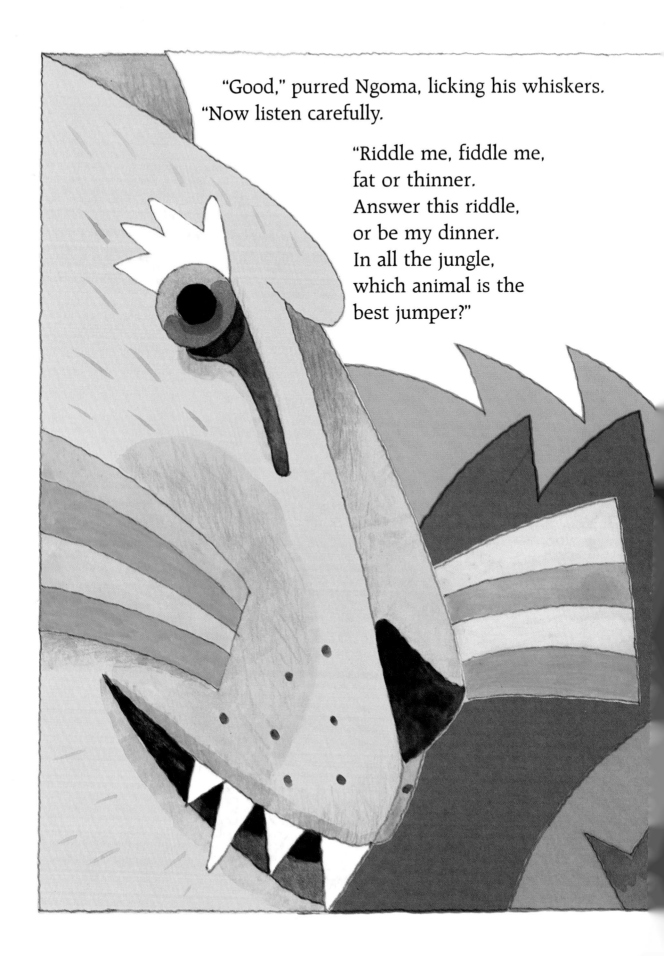

"Good," purred Ngoma, licking his whiskers. "Now listen carefully.

"Riddle me, fiddle me,
fat or thinner.
Answer this riddle,
or be my dinner.
In all the jungle,
which animal is the
best jumper?"

Jimjup's antenna trembled as he thought. "It could be the impala. It could be the leopard. But I think it's a cricket like me!"

"Wrong," replied Ngoma, pouncing on the cricket. "The best jumper in all the jungle is me. See!"

Not long after...*swesha, swesha, swesha...* winding down the jungle path came mamba.*

"Tell me, Msungu," Ngoma purred, "where are you going on this sun-hot evening?"

"Down to the Galana to drink the cool water," Msungu answered. "All day I've been gliding through the grass. I am very thirsty."

Ngoma stretched out across the path. "Do you like riddles, Msungu?"

"Very much," the mamba hissed.

"Good," purred Ngoma, picking his teeth. "Now listen carefully.

"Riddle me, fiddle me, fat or thinner.
Answer this riddle, or be my dinner.
In all the jungle, which animal has the most deadly bite?"

Msungu's tongue darted in and out as he thought. "It could be the crocodile. It could be the tsetse fly. But I think it's a mamba like me!"

"Wrong," replied Ngoma, snapping his jaws. "In all the jungle, the animal with the deadliest bite is me. See!"

Not long after...*tsip-sip, tsip-sip, tsip-sip*...
strutting down the jungle path came ostrich.
   "Tell me, Kikulu," Ngoma purred, "where
are you going on this sun-hot evening?"
   "Down to the Galana to drink the cool
water," Kikulu answered. "All day I've been
running in the sun. I am very thirsty."

Ngoma's tail brushed back and forth across the path. "Do you like riddles, Kikulu?"

"Yes." The ostrich nodded.

"Good," Ngoma grinned, rippling his muscles. "Now listen carefully.

"Riddle me, fiddle me, fat or thinner.
Answer this riddle, or be my dinner.
In all the jungle, which animal is
the fastest?

Kikulu's head bobbed up and down as she thought. "It could be the cheetah. It could be the gazelle. But I think it's an ostrich like me!"

"Wrong," replied Ngoma, leaping like lightning. "In all the jungle, the fastest animal is me. See!"

Not long after...*b'jom-bom*, *b'jom-bom*, *b'jom-bom*...rumbling down the jungle path came elephant.

"Tell me, Tutusk," Ngoma purred. "Where are you going on this sun-hot evening?

"Down to the Galana to drink the cool water," Tutusk answered. "All day I've been marching through the jungle. I am very thirsty."

Ngoma's claws flashed in and out. "Do you like riddles, Tutusk?"

"I do." The elephant blinked.

"Good," purred Ngoma, shaking his mane. "Now listen carefully.

"Riddle me, fiddle me, fat or thinner.
Answer this riddle, or be my dinner.
In all the jungle, which animal is
the loudest?"

Tutusk swayed back and forth as he thought. "It could be the baboon. It could be the hyena. But I think it's a trumpeting elephant like me!"

"Wrong," roared Ngoma so loudly the earth shook. "In all the jungle, the loudest animal is me. SEE!"

Now Ngoma was as full and round as the
moon above. Rolling to his feet, he lumbered
down the jungle path.

He had almost reached the river when he
heard...*chee, chee, chee*...up above in the
mimosa tree.

"Tell me, Ngoma," called Lobola the
monkey. "Where are you going on this moon-
bright night?"

"Down to the Galana to drink the cool
water, I've been asking riddles all day. I am
very thirsty."

"Riddles," laughed Lobola. "I know a very clever riddle."

"Then tell me," snarled Ngoma.

"I do not think you are smart enough to answer it," Lobola said, swinging by her tail.

Ngoma growled. Ngoma roared, "Tell me that riddle or be my dinner!"

"All right," agreed Lobola. "If you insist.

"Riddle me, fiddle me, lion so strong.
Answer my riddle, right or wrong.
In all the jungle, which animal can swing
the farthest on this vine?"

Ngoma thought long. Ngoma thought hard. But before he could answer, Lobola grabbed the vine and swung all the way across the Galana River.

"You may be the best jumper, biter, runner, and roared in all the jungle," Lobola laughed, "but you can *never* swing as far as I can."

Ngoma snapped and snarled and spat. "No monkey can outdo me. See!"

Snatching the vine, Ngoma leaped into the air. Over the cliff, past the riverbank, and high above the rushing rapids he sailed.

But that lion had eaten so much that not even the longest, strongest vine in all the jungle could hold him up for long.

The farther he swung, the thinner the vine stretched. Ngoma had nearly reached the other side when the vine stretched and stretched until KAPAP! It snapped in half.

With a mighty "AROARRR!" Ngoma tumbled down, down, deep into the muddy river, never to be seen again.

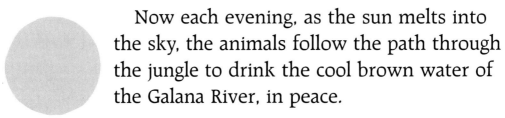

Now each evening, as the sun melts into the sky, the animals follow the path through the jungle to drink the cool brown water of the Galana River, in peace.

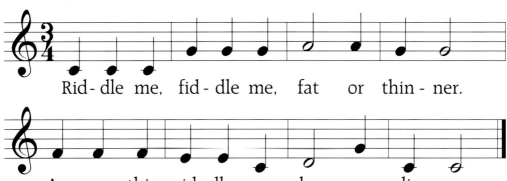

Rid - dle me, fid - dle me, fat or thin - ner.

An - swer this rid - dle, or be my din - ner.